BIGFOOT

monster
Chronicles

monster
Chronicles

BIGFOOT

Stephen Krensky

Lerner Publications Company · Minneapolis

Copyright © 2007 by Stephen Krensky

Lerner Publications Company
A division of Lerner Publishing Group
241 First Avenue North
Minneapolis, MN 55401 U.S.A.

Website address: www.lernerbooks.com

Library of Congress Cataloging-in-Publication Data

Krensky, Stephen.
    Bigfoot / Stephen Krensky.
        p. cm. — (Monster chronicles)
    Includes bibliographical references and index.
    ISBN-13: 978-0-8225-5925-2 (lib. bdg. : alk. paper)
    ISBN-10: 0-8225-5925-0 (lib. bdg. : alk. paper)
    1. Sasquatch—Juvenile literature. I. Title. II. Series.
    QL89.2.S2K74 2007
    001.944—dc22   2006000161

Manufactured in the United States of America
1 2 3 4 5 6 - JR - 12 11 10 09 08 07

TABLE OF CONTENTS

1 WHOSE FOOTPRINTS ARE THOSE, ANYWAY?

Everyone agrees that Bigfoot is a monster. Everyone agrees that he's hairy. Most of the time, everyone agrees that he's big—seven or more feet tall. He's also incredibly strong. And, of course, there's no question about his big feet.

What people don't agree about is whether Bigfoot really exists. And they've been arguing about this question for a while. For thousands of years, people have claimed to see big, hairy creatures living just outside the borders of civilization. Were they real? Or were they imaginary? Some people tried to find out. Others just shrugged. In places where people were worried about just finding enough food to eat, answering questions about Bigfoot didn't seem so important. Even if the creature

But times change. Life has grown more complicated, with more and more machines, scientific discoveries, and ways to get information. So people want to know more and more about the world around them, especially mysterious things.

People have reported seeing Bigfoot-type creatures all over the earth. In the United States, most sightings have occurred in California, Oregon, and Washington. Some people in Florida claim to have seen a small, extremely smelly version of Bigfoot. They call him the Skunk Ape. The Canadian provinces of Alberta and British Columbia are also hot spots for Bigfoot sightings. In Asia sightings have come from China, Mongolia, Tibet, and Nepal.

Some researchers have tried to connect the various stories from around the world. They hope to show that different Bigfoot sightings fit together as pieces of one big puzzle. They wonder if Bigfoot creatures from different places all belong to the same species. But Bigfoot creatures are like UFOs (unidentified flying objects). Many people claim to have seen them, but so far, no one has found proof that they exist.

Yeti means "magical creature" in Tibetan. Reports of a big, apelike creature have come from remote spots around the world.

WHAT'S IN A NAME?

For a creature that may or may not exist, Bigfoot has a lot of names. People in China call him the

English explorers who began visiting the Himalayas in the 1920s made the name Abominable Snowman popular.

Wildman. In Mongolia he is called the Alma. People in the Himalayas, a range of tall mountains in southern Asia, sometimes call him the Yeti. People in Tibet also use the name *metoh-kangmi.* It means "man-sized snow creature." But one English-language newspaper translated the term as Abominable (or horrible) Snowman.

In Canada Bigfoot is called Sasquatch. This Native American name means "hairy giant." The early Native Americans did not fear Sasquatch. They thought he was just another creature in the woods, like bears and deer. Native Americans respected Sasquatch's size and strength. For these same reasons, they kept their distance from him.

The first appearance of the name Bigfoot came in 1958. A northern California newspaper, the *Humboldt Times,* printed a story about large, mysterious footprints found near a construction site. These prints were far larger than any shoes on display in the Basketball Hall of Fame. Given the size of the prints, the name Bigfoot was a natural for the creature that made them. Were they real? Many people suspected a hoax, but nothing was ever proved. The name Bigfoot, however, was here to stay.

Phil Thompson measures a footprint he and his partner discovered near Coos Bay, Oregon, in 1976. The footprint was seventeen inches long and seven inches wide. Could it be Bigfoot?

DOES BIGFOOT HAVE A FAMILY TREE?

Whatever name you like, the creature is legendary. But unlike other monsters, he's legendary only because he's so hard to find. Nobody thinks Bigfoot is an alien from outer space. No one believes he is a leftover god from ancient Greece. People don't think Bigfoot is a

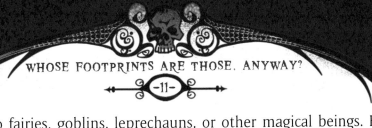

cousin to fairies, goblins, leprechauns, or other magical beings. He has no special powers. Sure, he's very big and strong. And he can live in harsh climates such as the Himalayas. But otherwise, he is perfectly ordinary.

Bigfoot doesn't resemble vampires or werewolves, either. According to stories, such creatures were once people—people who were turned into monsters by spells, potions, or changes of the moon. But no magic can turn someone into Bigfoot. If you look in the mirror and see a Bigfoot looking back, it's because you were born that way.

Those who believe in Bigfoot say he is as human as we are—or almost as human. But how did he come about? One popular answer is based on the theory of evolution. According to this theory, we modern humans are not

The snowy peaks of the Himalayas would provide a perfect place for the Yeti to live.

In the way some modern humans believe
in wild creatures such as Bigfoot, the ancient Greeks
believed in satyrs *(above)*. Satyrs looked like humans with some
animal body parts, such as horns and hooves. According to
ancient stories, satyrs liked to drink
wine and dance.

the same people we were thousands and thousands of years ago. In long-
ago days, several kinds of humanlike beings roamed the planet. Scientists
think that people like us—animals with the scientific name *Homo sapiens*—
won the battle for survival. Other beings gradually died out.

But what if they didn't die out—at least not completely? What if a few of them survived by hiding in icy mountains and other remote areas?

One group of early humans, the Neanderthals, shares some traits with Bigfoot. The Neanderthals lived in parts of Europe, Asia, and Africa. We can tell from their remains—their heavy bones and teeth—that they were very strong. Scientists think that the last Neanderthal died about thirty thousand years ago.

An artist's representation of what Neanderthals might have looked like. Some believers think that Bigfoot is a descendant of Neanderthals.

The Neanderthals got their name from the Neander Valley of Germany, where their bones (above) were first found in 1856.

But what if that isn't true? What if the descendants of Neanderthals are the Bigfoot creatures of modern times?

Proving that Bigfoot exists doesn't depend on finding one of the creatures alive—although clearly this would help. After all, there are no dinosaurs still roaming the earth. But we have plenty of evidence—bones and fossils—that dinosaurs once lumbered about. But no one has found any bones, teeth, or other signs of an ancient Bigfoot.

If Bigfoot and his family really are wandering around, you'd think that in an age of GPS (global positioning system), infrared night goggles, and high-powered binoculars, it would be fairly easy to find them.

Yet we have not discovered any sign of their campsites, their belongings, or the Bigfoot ancestors who died before them.

Nevertheless, Bigfoot has many enthusiastic fans and believers. They write Bigfoot books and create Bigfoot websites. They put a great amount of time and energy into trying to prove that Bigfoot exists. Doubters ask the believers: Where could these creatures possibly be hiding to escape all modern detection systems? But doubters don't bother the true believers. Believers say that Bigfoot lives in parts of the earth's vast forests and rugged mountains that have never been completely checked.

In 1999 the Chinese Academy of Sciences put out a report that the Yeti did not exist. This report said that 95 percent of Yeti sightings and stories had been proven untrue. However, in the eyes of true believers, this still leaves 5 percent of the stories unexplained. So their hope remains alive. And the hunt for Bigfoot goes on.

2 BIGFOOT, FRONT AND CENTER

For all the stories surrounding the mysterious Bigfoot, he seems to be a pretty modest monster. You don't see Bigfoot tooting his own horn or bragging about his abilities. And Bigfoot doesn't intrude on other people's lives, either. He doesn't borrow stuff without asking. Bigfoot minds his own business.

In some ways, Bigfoot is similar to Nessie, the sea monster said to live in Loch Ness, a lake in Scotland. Like Nessie, Bigfoot *could exist* without breaking the laws of the natural world. That is, it's perfectly believable that a big unknown animal could live in the woods and mountains. But *could exist* and *does exist* are two very different things.

Florida's Skunk Ape is said to be much smaller than other Bigfoot creatures—only four or five feet tall. This photo was taken in Florida in 2000. The creature was seen taking apples from the back porch of an elderly couple's house.

WHAT DOES BIGFOOT LOOK LIKE?

As the name suggests, Bigfoot has big feet. However, his feet are only one part of his overall size. Those who claim to have seen him say Bigfoot can weigh up to five hundred pounds and that he stands seven or eight feet tall. He also has broad shoulders and a thick body, kind of like a football player wearing several sets of padding.

All of this bulk is covered in fur. The color ranges from reddish brown to black. (A graying Bigfoot seems to be especially rare.) He has a stooped posture, with long arms that hang to his knees. He walks upright, on two feet. His palms, the bottom of his feet, his nose, and his forehead are hairless. He has a flat nose, a sloping forehead, and ridges above his eyes. In many ways, he looks like a gorilla wearing a thick winter coat of fur.

Bigfoot also resembles a Wookiee from the *Star Wars* movies (1977–2005). But unlike the Wookiee Chewbacca, who was a skilled space pilot, Bigfoot is thought to have limited intelligence. How do we know? Observers say that Bigfoot acts like a wild animal. He lives a simple existence, without clothing, tools, or houses. But Bigfoot can't be too dumb. He's obviously clever enough to avoid discovery by humans.

Naturally, keeping such a big guy happy requires a lot of food. Apparently, Bigfoot is not fussy in his eating habits. He seems to eat a little bit of everything. Yetis living in the mountains of Tibet eat whatever is

Pictures of the Yeti appear in some Tibetan religious artwork. But the Tibetans do not worship the Yeti as a god.

Chewbacca, the Wookiee pilot in *Star Wars*, looks something like Bigfoot—big and furry.

Russian researcher Maya Bykova, who died in 1996, reported a Bigfoot sighting in western Siberia—a remote region of Russia—in 1988. She devoted much of her career to looking for proof of Bigfoot's existence.

handy—mice, berries, roots, and sometimes sheep. It is unclear if Bigfoot cooks his meat, but he does not seem to be a fancy chef. He doesn't use pots and pans or forks and knives.

Bigfoot is probably shy. Or at least he avoids the spotlight. He doesn't seem to be angry or cruel, because few people have reported a Bigfoot attack. Bigfoot does not act fierce like a wolf or a bear. He does not have fangs or claws. He has a peaceful nature, which probably explains why Bigfoot observers have a high survival rate.

CRYPTOZOOLOGY

The study of fantastic creatures that have not been proven to exist is called cryptozoology. The name comes from the words *crypto*, meaning "hidden," and *zoology*, the study of animals. In addition to Bigfoot, cryptozoologists are looking for several other legendary creatures. The most famous is the Loch Ness Monster *(above)*. Generally, scientists who study animals do not respect the work of cryptozoologists.

LIVING THE SIMPLE LIFE

Bigfoot lives simply. According to believers, there are no Bigfoot buildings, inventions, or laws. Bigfoot apparently lives in caves or perhaps trees. There's no sign of anything else he might use for a home. One thing that all Bigfoot observers agree on is that Bigfoot doesn't wear clothes. Bigfoot is not making any fashion statements. No one has found signs of Bigfoot cars, bicycles, or backyard toys, either. It seems that Bigfoot society is made up of hunters and gatherers, creatures who live off the land.

And how many Bigfoot creatures are there? It's hard to say. But there probably aren't too many. In fact, it's hard to imagine more than a few in any one place. If the

Could Bigfoot be lurking somewhere in the thick forests of the western United States and Canada?

In 1962 a Chinese newspaper reported that Chinese soldiers had killed and eaten a Yeti in a remote part of China. However, no one followed up to find out if the story was true.

Bigfoot population was bigger than that, they wouldn't be able to stay hidden for long. Of course, it helps that the creatures stick to remote areas. Yetis live in mountain caves from 12,000 to 20,000 feet above sea level. In the northern United States and Canada, Bigfoot and Sasquatch stay in the thick forests, where only loggers go from one year to the next. In Florida, Skunk Apes stay hidden in swamps.

All this isolation keeps Bigfoot safely away from human settlements. It makes him hard to find. But being isolated is good too. Because if there's one thing that everyone who has seen Bigfoot up close agrees on, it's that he smells bad.

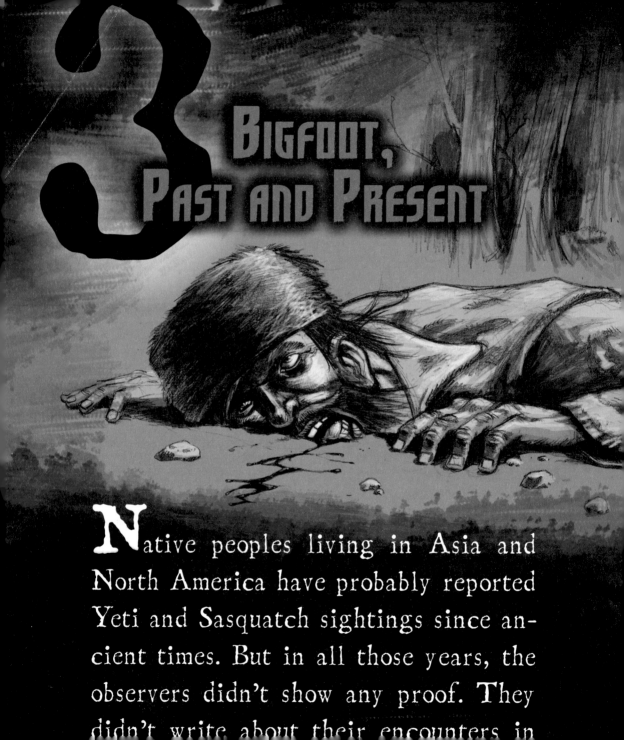

3 Bigfoot, Past and Present

Native peoples living in Asia and North America have probably reported Yeti and Sasquatch sightings since ancient times. But in all those years, the observers didn't show any proof. They didn't write about their encounters in

books or newspapers. They just told stories about what they had seen.

In the days before cameras, television, and the Internet, a story about a Sasquatch or Yeti was enough evidence for most people. People who heard such a story simply assumed it was true. But in the 1800s, explorers, hunters, and adventurers began to travel to the earth's remote regions. Many of these travelers wrote about their experiences in diaries, letters, and books. Some of these writings told about Bigfoot sightings.

One account came from David Thompson. He was an animal trapper who crossed the Rocky Mountains near Alberta, Canada, in the early 1800s. He recorded this entry in his journal:

> Continuing our journey in the afternoon we came on the track of a large animal. The snow about six inches deep on the ice; I measured it; four large toes each of four inches in length to each a short claw . . . the length fourteen inches, by eight inches in breadth.

The Native Americans traveling with Thompson were sure a Sasquatch had made the tracks. Thompson wasn't so sure. When he suggested that an old bear might have left the prints, the Native Americans disagreed.

Later in the 1800s, Theodore Roosevelt (a rancher at the time and later president of the United States) told a story he had heard from an old hunter named Baumann. In his younger days, Baumann had trapped

Teddy Roosevelt (*above*) shared a report of a Bigfoot encounter told by a fellow hunter. Roosevelt later became president of the United States.

animals with a friend in the Rocky Mountains. One day the men returned to their camp and found it had been destroyed. Who or what had done the damage? The footprints left behind made the trappers think of a bear—but a bear that walked on two legs. The next day, they went trapping again. And again when they returned, they found their camp destroyed. That night they heard something stomping around outside their tent. Baumann fired a shot from his rifle, and the intruder ran off. The following morning, Baumann went alone to collect some traps. When he returned, he found an unpleasant surprise. His fellow trapper was dead, his neck broken. Baumann was a tough mountain man, but he didn't wait to make his next move. He fled.

Another story came from the town of Yale, British Columbia. Residents there had caught an apelike creature. In an article dated July 4, 1884, a local newspaper reported the capture:

"Jacko," as the creature has been called by his captors, is something of the gorilla type, standing about four feet seven inches in height and weighing 127 pounds. He has long, black, strong hair about one inch long. His forearm is much longer than a man's forearm, and he possesses extraordinary strength, as he will take hold of a stick and break it by wrenching or twisting it, which no man living could break in the same way.

This story was specific. But reporters never followed up on it. No further word of Jacko ever appeared in print. Was Jacko really a new kind of creature? Was he a chimpanzee that had escaped from a nearby circus? More

likely, the whole story was a hoax made up by the newspaper. Newspapers of the time sometimes got creative to amuse their readers.

More sightings came from Asia. In 1889 Major L. A. Waddell, a British explorer in the Himalayas, was the first European to report seeing Yeti footprints in the snow. Waddell didn't know they were Yeti footprints. He only knew they were big and mysterious. But his local guides said the tracks had been made by a Yeti. Waddell assumed the guides knew what they were talking about and took their word. But it's possible the guides were just having a little fun at Waddell's expense.

Sightings of Yetis increased in the 1920s, when American and European mountain climbers began taking more trips to the Himalayas. One foreign visitor who came upon a Yeti said it was unclear who was more afraid at that moment—he or the Yeti.

The Cardiff giant (*below*) was discovered in 1869 in Cardiff, New York. The giant became an overnight sensation, drawing crowds—and money— from around the United States. Two weeks after its discovery, it was exposed as a fake.

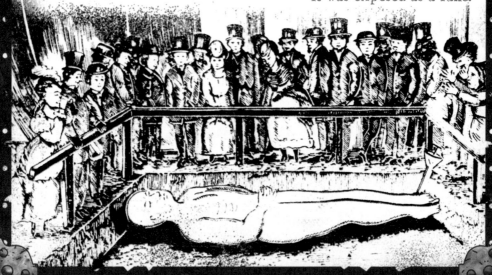

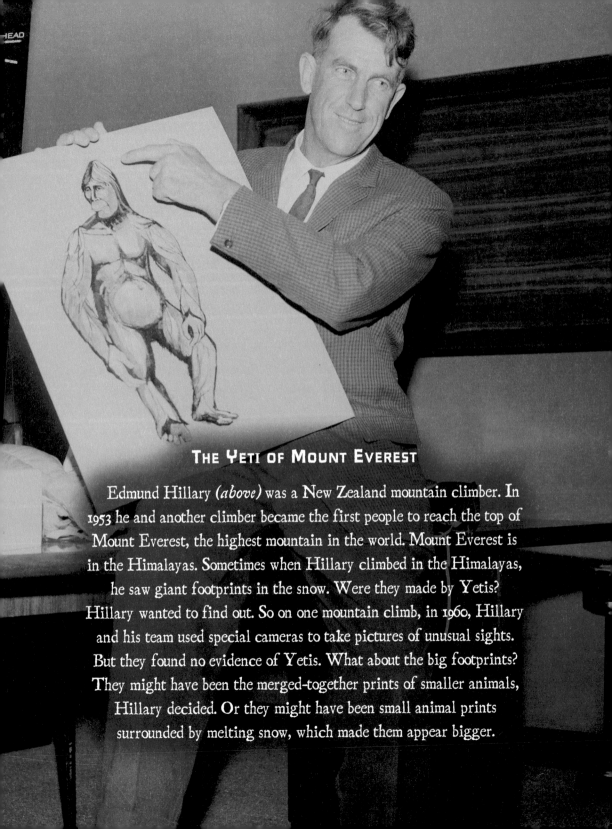

The Yeti of Mount Everest

Edmund Hillary (*above*) was a New Zealand mountain climber. In
1953 he and another climber became the first people to reach the top of
Mount Everest, the highest mountain in the world. Mount Everest is
in the Himalayas. Sometimes when Hillary climbed in the Himalayas,
he saw giant footprints in the snow. Were they made by Yetis?
Hillary wanted to find out. So on one mountain climb, in 1960, Hillary
and his team used special cameras to take pictures of unusual sights.
But they found no evidence of Yetis. What about the big footprints?
They might have been the merged-together prints of smaller animals,
Hillary decided. Or they might have been small animal prints
surrounded by melting snow, which made them appear bigger.

BIGFOOT OR BIGFEET?

Usually, people report seeing just one Bigfoot. But doesn't Bigfoot get lonely? Is there a Mrs. Bigfoot? Are there baby Bigfoots—or Bigfeet? Does Bigfoot have a family? It all depends on whom you ask. If you had asked Albert Ostman, a Canadian lumberjack of the early 1900s, the answer would have been yes.

In 1924 Ostman was doing a little digging for gold near Vancouver Island off the west coast of Canada. He claimed that a Bigfoot family—

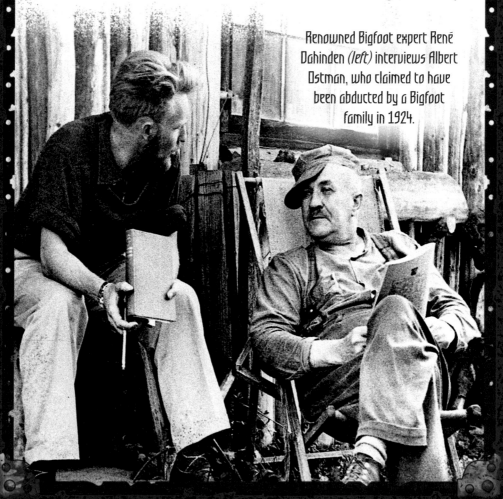

Renowned Bigfoot expert René Dahinden *(left)* interviews Albert Ostman, who claimed to have been abducted by a Bigfoot family in 1924.

a father, a mother, a son, and a daughter—captured him there. The family appeared to be vegetarians. They ate only roots and plants, which was probably lucky for Ostman. After about a week, Ostman was able to slip away.

In the 1920s, miners in the state of Washington told of mysterious creatures throwing rocks at their cabins in the middle of the night. They also claimed to find giant footprints outside the cabins the next morning.

Ostman could not explain why he had been taken prisoner or why he was allowed to escape. In fact, he didn't even tell anyone about his capture for thirty-three years. He was afraid everyone would think he was crazy. Ostman was probably right to keep quiet. Often nonbelievers make fun of people who say they've seen Bigfoot.

HOAXES AND HEARSAY

Nonbelievers are also suspicious of such hoaxes. Plenty of people have created Bigfoot hoaxes over the years. Some people have made movies of friends running around in hairy costumes, then claimed they've captured Bigfoot on film. Other people have made large, fake footprints in snow or mud.

In the 1960s, exhibitors displayed a creature called the Iceman at carnivals in the midwestern United States. The manlike figure was encased in a block of ice, which kept him from being seen clearly. But the resemblance to Bigfoot was noticeable. It would have made sense to melt the ice for a closer look. But before an examination could be

René Dahinden *(left)* and Bigfoot filmmaker Roger Patterson *(right)* hold casts of two footprints found in Bluff Creek, California.

made, exhibitors claimed that the Iceman had mysteriously disappeared. Was the Iceman display a hoax? You be the judge.

Among the most famous hoaxers was Ray Wallace, who once ran a construction company that built logging roads in California. Wallace started out small, creating fake Bigfoot footprints. He later made films and photographs showing creatures that he claimed to be Bigfoot. Wallace's son later told the truth about his father's hoaxes.

In 1967 Roger Patterson shot a home movie near Bluff Creek in northern California. The film showed a creature that Patterson claimed to be

People often gather at conferences to discuss Bigfoot sightings. They offer theories about Bigfoot's origins and talk about how Bigfoot and his relatives could survive in modern times. So far, all the participants have been strictly human.

Bigfoot. Critics believe that the "Bigfoot" in the film was just a man running around in a hairy suit. They say Patterson created the film to help sell his book, *Do Abominable Snowmen of America Really Exist?* But Patterson, who died in 1972, stood by his story.

In modern times, of course, a proven Bigfoot sighting would make instant news around the world. The days of a sighting gradually making its way back to civilization through word of mouth are long gone. Within hours of such news, media helicopters would land at the spot of the sighting. Reporters would rush to the scene. Movie offers and multimillion-dollar book deals would follow. If Bigfoot isn't interested in these things, he would do well to keep his head down.

Four stills from Roger Patterson's Bigfoot movie, shot on October 20, 1967, at Bluff Creek, California

BIGFOOT STEPS OUT

Since Bigfoot has been so hard to pin down, his appearance and personality are somewhat vague. But that hasn't kept moviemakers from giving him star qualities. The British company Hammer Film Productions (which later produced a number of Dracula and Frankenstein movies) made one of the first attempts to turn Bigfoot into a movie star.

Hammer's movie, *The Abominable Snowman of the Himalayas* (1957), centered on a fictional Yeti hunt. A conflict arises between two of the hunters. One wants to simply find the Yeti. The other wants to capture the creature and make money from it.

The Abominable Snowman, shown here in a tight spot, hit the big screen in 1957.

The Legend of Boggy Creek (1972) took a different slant. This "mock-umentary," or fake nonfiction film, concerns a Bigfoot-like creature that lives in the woods in southwestern Arkansas. He's known as the Fouke Monster, and he kills chickens and other farm animals. He also smells terrible and makes strange noises. The movie follows the work of investigators, who search the area and question local residents.

One of the most famous movies about Bigfoot is *Harry and the Hendersons* (1987). The plot follows the ordinary Henderson family, whose car accidentally hits an animal on the way back from a camping trip. But this is no deer in the road. It's a giant hairy creature. The

Hendersons think he's dead. They take him home, only to discover that their car had merely stunned him. Luckily for them, he is friendly and doesn't hold a grudge. The rest of the movie concerns the Hendersons' efforts to keep Harry (as they have named the creature) safe from the police and a Bigfoot hunter.

Walt Disney Pictures produced a movie called *Bigfoot* (1987), in which two kids try to save an innocent Sasquatch from being captured.

Less lovable but more traditional is the Abominable Snowman in *A Goofy Movie* (1995) from Walt Disney Pictures. Here, Goofy and his nephew Max, in the middle of a cross-country trip, come across Bigfoot while camping. Goofy films Bigfoot with his video camera, thinking he will be famous for getting proof of the hard-to-find creature's

Having a Bigfoot around the house makes for trouble in the Henderson family.

Harry and the Hendersons was the basis for a 1991–1993 TV series with the same name.

existence. But Bigfoot has other ideas. He destroys the film, leaving Goofy—as so many Bigfoot observers before him—with nothing to show for his efforts.

BIGFOOT, SMALL SCREEN

Television has examined Bigfoot several times too. In the animated television special *Rudolph the Red-Nosed Reindeer* (1964), it isn't enough that poor Rudolph has a very shiny nose. It isn't enough that all the other reindeer tease him and won't let him play in their reindeer games. On top of all that, an Abominable Snowman looms

In *Rudolph the Red-Nosed Reindeer*, the Abominable Snowman was hairy but not all that scary.

in Rudolph's future. Luckily, the snowman's reputation turns out to be much fiercer than the snowman himself. The show's stop-action animation keeps all the characters looking like toys. Even a grouchy Abominable Snowman isn't very scary.

The wrestler-turned-actor André the Giant played Bigfoot in two episodes of TV's 1970s action series *The Six Million Dollar Man.* In these shows, Bigfoot turns out to come from

At seven feet tall, André the Giant was a good choice for playing Bigfoot on TV.

another planet. He is a bionic creature (a mixture of natural, mechanical, and electronic parts) brought to earth by aliens.

The cartoon series *Jonny Quest,* which first aired in the 1960s, featured Yetis in one episode. In this show, bad guys who want to take over a Himalayan village put on Yeti costumes to scare the villagers. They are defeated, partly through Jonny's efforts and partly through the efforts of real Yetis, who don't like seeing fakers ruin their good name.

In an updated 1990s version of *Jonny Quest,* Jonny's father, Dr. Quest, goes missing on an expedition to find the Yeti. Jonny searches for his father while trying to stop another scientist who is determined to capture a Yeti— dead or alive.

Johnny Quest and his, dog Bandit, had an encounter with the Yeti.

In *Monsters, Inc.* (2001), the large, blue, furry monster Sulley is a creature in the Bigfoot tradition.

WHERE DOES BIGFOOT GO FROM HERE?

What does the future hold for Bigfoot? Nobody has a firm answer yet. For the moment, Bigfoot has much in common with aliens from outer space. Lots of people believe in them. Lots of people claim to have seen them or to have evidence that they exist. But the official proof—that all-important interview on the evening news—has not yet appeared.

Why can't anyone find Bigfoot? Maybe being hard to find is just part of Bigfoot's master plan. He may want to stay hidden and keep everyone guessing about his existence. Unlike the fairy Tinker Bell in *Peter Pan,* Bigfoot may *not* want people to believe in him. And in that case, he and his Bigfoot relatives will be just fine.

GLOSSARY OF MYSTERIOUS ANIMALS

Bigfoot is just one of many mysterious animals that may or may not exist. Here are a few more:

Chupacabra: Sighted in Puerto Rico, Mexico, and parts of the mainland United States, Chupacabra is a lizardlike being that drinks the blood of animals, especially goats. Its name is Spanish for "goat sucker." According to some descriptions, Chupacabra stands three to four feet tall. It has leathery, greenish gray skin and large fangs, and it hops on two feet like a kangaroo. Some believers think Chupacabras are aliens from outer space.

Goatman: As its name implies, Goatman is a human-goat combination. It has the legs and feet of a goat, the upper body of a man, and horns on its head. According to one witness, the Goatman stands seven feet tall. Some people think it is a relative of Bigfoot. It also resembles the satyrs of Greek mythology and the ancient Greek god Pan.

Jersey Devil: The Jersey Devil makes its home in the Pine Barrens in southern New Jersey. The strange beast is said to have a long neck, wings, hooves, and glowing red eyes. It stands between three and seven feet tall. For hundreds of years, people in New Jersey have reported seeing the creature, which is said to attack both humans and animals. New Jersey's professional hockey team, the New Jersey Devils, is named for this scary creature.

Kraken: Kraken is a sea monster said to live off the coasts of Norway and Iceland in northern Europe. Sailors in this region have reported Kraken sightings for hundreds of years. The beast resembles a giant octopus, and it is large enough to pull a big ship to the bottom of the ocean. Scientists think that Kraken stories might come from sightings of the giant squid, a real-life animal that lives deep in the ocean.

Loch Ness Monster: Along with Bigfoot, the Loch Ness Monster is the most famous mysterious animal. Nicknamed Nessie, the monster lives in Loch Ness, a lake in northern Scotland. Nessie sightings began in the 1930s. Since then, the monster has become famous. Teams of scientists have explored the lake with underwater cameras and high-tech equipment. Tourists also come to Loch Ness to try to catch a glimpse of Nessie. Apparently, Nessie has flippers, humps on its back, and a long slender neck. Some believers think Nessie is descended from the plesiosaur, a prehistoric reptile.

Mothman: Mothman sightings began in the 1960s. According to eyewitnesses, the creature looks like a huge man, with glowing red eyes and big wings on its back. Most Mothman sightings come from West Virginia. Observers have seen the creature perched on the ground and soaring through the sky. Many people believe the observers. But others say the observers actually saw a large bird, such as the great horned owl.

Ogopogo: Like Nessie, the Ogopogo is a large lake monster. It lives in Lake Okanagan in British Columbia, Canada. The creature is said to resemble a large, snakelike whale. In earlier centuries, Native Americans in the region spoke of the "great beast in the lake" and the "snake in the lake." Modern people continue to search for the creature. One film shows a dark object moving through the lake near the shore. Many people think the object is Ogopogo.

Thunderbird: The Thunderbird is an enormous bird with a wingspan around twenty-five feet—the size of a small airplane. The bird has its roots in Native American folklore. It resembles a pterodactyl, a prehistoric flying reptile. Reportedly, a Thunderbird once grabbed a small boy in Illinois and carried him through the air. Other Thunderbird sightings have come from Alaska, Washington, Utah, Idaho, and Ohio.

SOURCE NOTES

26 Don Hunter and René Dahinden, *Sasquatch/Bigfoot: The Search for North America's Incredible Creature* (Buffalo: Firefly Books, 1993), 17.

27 Ibid., 23.

SELECTED BIBLIOGRAPHY

Coleman, Loren, and Patrick Huyghe. *The Field Guide to Bigfoot, Yeti and Other Mystery Primates Worldwide.* New York: Avon Books, 1999.

Hunter, Don, and René Dahinden. *Sasquatch/Bigfoot: The Search for North America's Incredible Creature.* Buffalo: Firefly Books, 1993.

Napier, John. *Bigfoot: The Yeti and Sasquatch in Myth and Reality.* New York: E. P. Dutton, 1973.

Place, Marian T. *On the Track of Bigfoot.* New York: Pocket Books, 1974.

Pyle, Robert Michael. *Where Bigfoot Walks: Crossing the Dark Divide.* New York: Mariner Books, 1997.

Shackley, Myra. *Still Living? Yetis, Sasquatch and the Neanderthal Enigma.* New York: Thames and Hudson, 1983.

FURTHER READING AND WEBSITES

Bigfoot Archive

http://www.bigfootarchive.com

This site is dedicated to all things Bigfoot, including articles, movies, books, and pictures.

Calhoun, Mary. *The Night the Monster Came.* New York: William Morrow, 1982. In this novel, when Andy finds really big footprints in the snow, he jumps to the conclusion that Bigfoot is somewhere in the neighborhood.

Cohen, Daniel. *Monster Hunting Today.* New York: Dodd, Mean and Company, 1983. The author describes the search for monsters around the world, including Bigfoot and his kin.

Coleman, Loren, and Jerome Clark. *Cryptozoology A to Z: The Encyclopedia of Loch Monsters, Sasquatch, Chupacabras, and Other Authentic Mysteries of Nature*. New York: Fireside, 1999. This handy reference book explores dozens of mysterious creatures and the people who search for them.

Herbst, Judith. *Monsters*. Minneapolis: Lerner Publications Company, 2005. Herbst recounts the ledgends and examines the myths surrounding several monsters, including Bigfoot and the Loch Ness Monster.

Innes, Brian. *Giant Humanlike Beasts*. Austin, TX: Raintree Steck-Vaughn, 1999. The author examines the Abominable Snowman, the Wildman of China, the Mongolian Alma, Bigfoot of North America, and other creatures.

Sasquatch Information Society
http://www.bigfootinfo.org
Sasquatch fans will find a host of information here, including events, links, photos, and a sighting database.

Smith, Roland. *Sasquatch*. New York: Hyperion, 1999. In this novel for young readers, thirteen-year-old Dylan joins his father on a search to find a Sasquatch.

MOVIES

The Abominable Snowman. Troy, MI: Anchor Bay Entertainment, 2000. This 1957 film, originally titled *The Abominable Snowman of the Himalayas*, recounts the adventures and struggles of a team of Yeti hunters.

Ancient Mysteries: Bigfoot. New York: A&E Home Video, 2005. This documentary film examines the Bigfoot legend and controversy. The narrator is former *Star Trek* actor Leonard Nimoy.

Harry and the Hendersons. Universal City, CA: Amblin Entertainment, Universal Pictures, 1987. This popular movie about a family-friendly Bigfoot is available for home viewing on DVD.

INDEX

ABOUT THE AUTHOR

Stephen Krensky is the author of many fiction and nonfiction books for children, including titles in the On My Own Folklore series and *Frankenstein*, *Werewolves*, *Dragons*, *Vampires*, and *The Mummy*. When he isn't hunched over his computer, he makes school visits and teaches writing workshops. In his free time, he enjoys playing tennis and softball and reading books by other people. Krensky lives in Massachusetts with his wife, Joan, and their family.

PHOTO ACKNOWLEDGMENTS

The images in this book are used with the permission of: © HAMMER/The Kobal Collection, pp. 2–3, 36; © Richard Svensson/Fortean Picture Library, p. 8; © Bettmann/CORBIS, pp. 10, 28, 29; © age fotostock/SuperStock, pp. 11, 22; © Fortean Picture Library, pp. 12, 13, 18; © Pascal Goetgheluck/Photo Researchers, Inc., p. 14; *Star Wars: Episode V—The Empire Strikes Back* © 1980 and 1997 Lucasfilm Ltd. & ™. All rights reserved. Used under authorization. Unauthorized duplication is a violation of applicable law. COURTESY OF LUCASFILM LTD., p. 19; © Keystone/Getty Images, p. 21; Library of Congress, p. 26 (LC-USZ62-23232); © René Dahinden/Fortean Picture Library, pp. 30, 32, 33 (all); Courtesy of Universal Studios Licensing LLLP. Image provided by Photofest, p. 37; © Todd Strand/Independent Picture Service, p. 38; © Hanna-Barbera Productions/Photofest, p. 39; © ABC/Photofest, p. 40. Illustrations by Bill Hauser, pp. 1, 6–7, 15, 16–17, 20, 24–25, 34–35. All page backgrounds illustrated by Bill Hauser.

Cover illustration: Bill Hauser.